baby einstein®

The ABCs of ART
N–Z

The WALT DISNEP Company

Fine Art Credits:

Le Domaine d'Amheim (The Amheim Estate), by Rene Magritte (1898–1967), C. Hersovici, Brussels/Artists Rights Society (ARS), New York, transparency R. Magritte-ADAGP/Art Resource, New York • *Octopus*, by Alexander Calder (1898–1976), Estate of Alexander Calder/Artists Rights Society (ARS), transparency, Art Resource, New York • *Peacock*, Anonymous, c. 1830, transparency, Victoria and Albert Museum, London/Art Resource, New York • *The Ermine Portrait*, by Nicholas Hillard (1547–1619), transparency, Victoria and Albert Museum, London/Art Resource, New York • *Dream of a Storm at Dawn*, by Charles E. Burchfield (1893–1967), transparency, Art Resource, New York • *Winter Landscape (February)*, by Lucas van Valckenborch (1530–1597), transparency, Erich Lessing/Art Resource, New York • *Buchenwald (Beech Trees)*, by Gustav Klimt (1862–1918), Erich Lessing/Art Resource, New York • *Children at the Ice Cream Stand*, by William H. Johnson (1901–1970), Smithsonian American Art Museum, Washington D.C./Art Resource, New York • *Rustic Violinist with Little Girl*, by Eastman Johnson (1824–1906), transparency, Art Resource, New York • *Pileated Woodpecker*, by John J. Audubon (1785–1851), transparency, Victoria and Albert Museum, London/Art Resource, New York • *Fay Ray X Ray*, by William Wegman (b. 1943) ©1994 William Wegman, reprinted by permission • *Study for Homage to the Square: Departing in Yellow*, by Joseph Albers (1888–1976), The Josef and Anni Albers Foundation/Artists Rights Society (ARS), transparency, Tate Gallery, London/Art Resource, New York • *Grevy's Zebra*, by Andy Warhol (1928–1987), The Andy Warhol Foundation for the Visual Arts/Artists Rights Society (ARS), New York, courtesy Ronald Feldman FineArts, Inc./Art Resource, New York, transparency, The Andy Warhol Foundation, Inc./Art Resource, New York

Hyperion Books for Children, New York
Copyright © 2004 by The Baby Einstein Company, LLC.
All Rights Reserved.
Baby Einstein and the Boy's Head Logo are trademarks of The Baby Einstein Company, LLC. All Rights Reserved.
EINSTEIN and ALBERT EINSTEIN are trademarks of The Hebrew University of Jerusalem. All Rights Reserved.
For information address Hyperion Books for Children, 114 Fifth Avenue, New York, New York 10011-5690.
Printed in China
Library of Congress Cataloging Card Number on file.
ISBN 0-7868-3808-6

Visit www.hyperionbooksforchildren.com and www.babyeinstein.com

Great Minds Start Little.™

nest

N is for nest.

How many eggs are in this nest?

Look carefully. Can you find the outline of a bird with spread-open wings?

octopus

O is for octopus.

What four colors do you see in this print?

Which of the objects do you think looks most like an octopus?

Oo

Pp

peacock

P is for peacock.

What do you think this peacock's feathers feel like?

What colors and shapes do you see in this bird?

queen

Q is for queen.

How can you tell that the woman in this painting is a queen?

Judging from her expression, how do you think the queen is feeling?

Rr

rainbow

R is for rainbow.

What colors do you see in the rainbow?

Can you see signs that some trees have been cut down?

snow

S is for snow.

If you could enter this painting, what might you hear? How might you feel?

What clues tell you that this is a scene from a long time ago?

trees

***T* is for trees.**

What time of year do you think it is in this painting?

What animals do you think live in this forest?

Uu

umbrella

U is for umbrella.

Why is the man standing under an umbrella?

Where do you think this scene takes place?

violin

V is for violin.

What clues tell you this scene takes place outdoors?

What song do you imagine the man is playing for the little girl?

Ww

woodpeckers

_W_ is for woodpeckers.

How many woodpeckers can you count on the tree?

Look carefully. Do you see a little worm?

X ray

X is for X ray.

If you could name this dog, what would you call her?

Can you point to the X ray of the dog's spine?

yellow

Y is for yellow.

How many different colored squares are in this painting?

Can you think of three things that are yellow?

Zz

zebra

Z is for zebra.

What colors do you see that are not found on real zebras?

Are the zebra's stripes in perfectly straight lines?